BRIGHT IDEA BOOKS

LeBRON James

by Laura Price Steele

CAPSTONE PRESS
a capstone imprint

Bright Ideas is published by Capstone Press, an imprint of Capstone.
1710 Roe Crest Drive
North Mankato, Minnesota 56003
www.capstonepub.com

Library of Congress Cataloging-in-Publication Data
Names: Steele, Laura Price, author.
Title: LeBron James / Laura Price Steele.
Description: North Mankato, Minnesota : Capstone Press, [2020] | Series: Influential People | Includes index. | Audience: Grades 4-6
Identifiers: LCCN 2019029348 (print) | LCCN 2019029349 (ebook) | ISBN 9781543590746 (hardcover) | ISBN 9781496665843 (paperback) | ISBN 9781543590753 (ebook)
Subjects: LCSH: James, LeBron—Juvenile literature. | Basketball players—United States Biography—Juvenile literature.
Classification: LCC GV884.J36 S74 2020 (print) | LCC GV884.J36 (ebook) | DDC 796.323092 [B]—dc23
LC record available at https://lccn.loc.gov/2019029348
LC ebook record available at https://lccn.loc.gov/2019029349

Photo Credits
Alamy: Allstar Picture Library, 10–11; AP Images: Bruce Schwartzman, 13, Gene J. Puskar, 5, Marcio Jose Sanchez, cover, Phil Long, 26, Tony Dejak, 17; Icon Sportswire: Ringo Chiu/Zuma Press, 18; iStockphoto, kali9, 31; Newscom: David Richard/USA Today Sports, 6–7, Ed Suba Jr./KRT, 14, Michael Chritton/Akron Beacon Journal/TNS, 25; Shutterstock Images: Henryk Sadura, 8–9, Kathy Hutchins, 22, 28, Tinseltown, 21
Design Elements: Shutterstock Images

Editorial Credits
Editor: Charly Haley; Designer: Laura Graphenteen; Production Specialist: Colleen McLaren

All internet sites appearing in back matter were available and accurate when this book was sent to press.

Printed in the United States 4975

TABLE OF CONTENTS

CHAPTER 1

HOMETOWN Hero

LeBron James rode in a car in a **parade**. People lined the sidewalk to watch. They cheered for James.

Cleveland, Ohio, was celebrating. It was June 2016. The Cleveland Cavaliers were champions. They had just won the National Basketball Association (NBA) championship. James smiled. He waved to the crowd.

James waved to his fans during a parade in Cleveland.

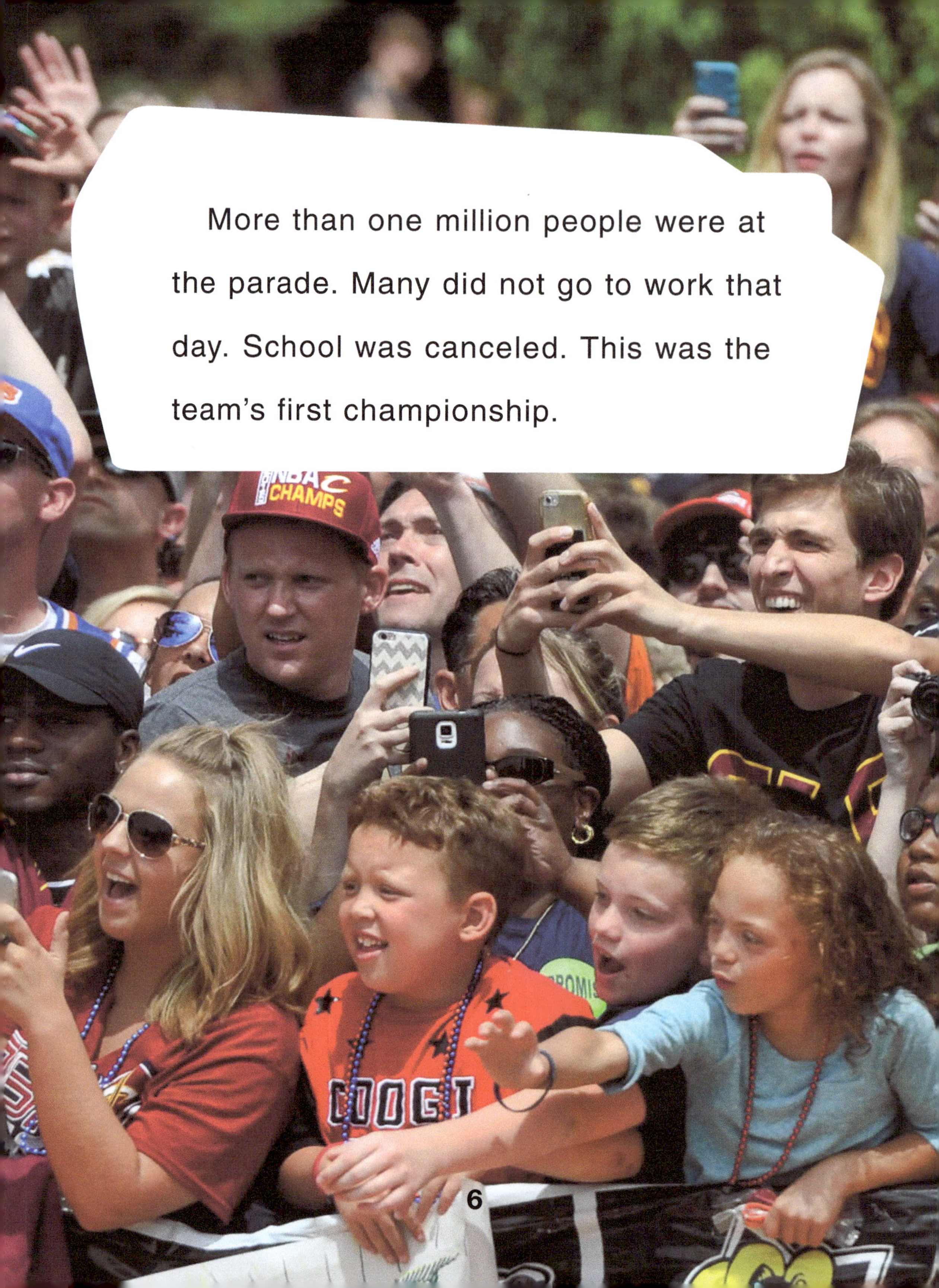

More than one million people were at the parade. Many did not go to work that day. School was canceled. This was the team's first championship.

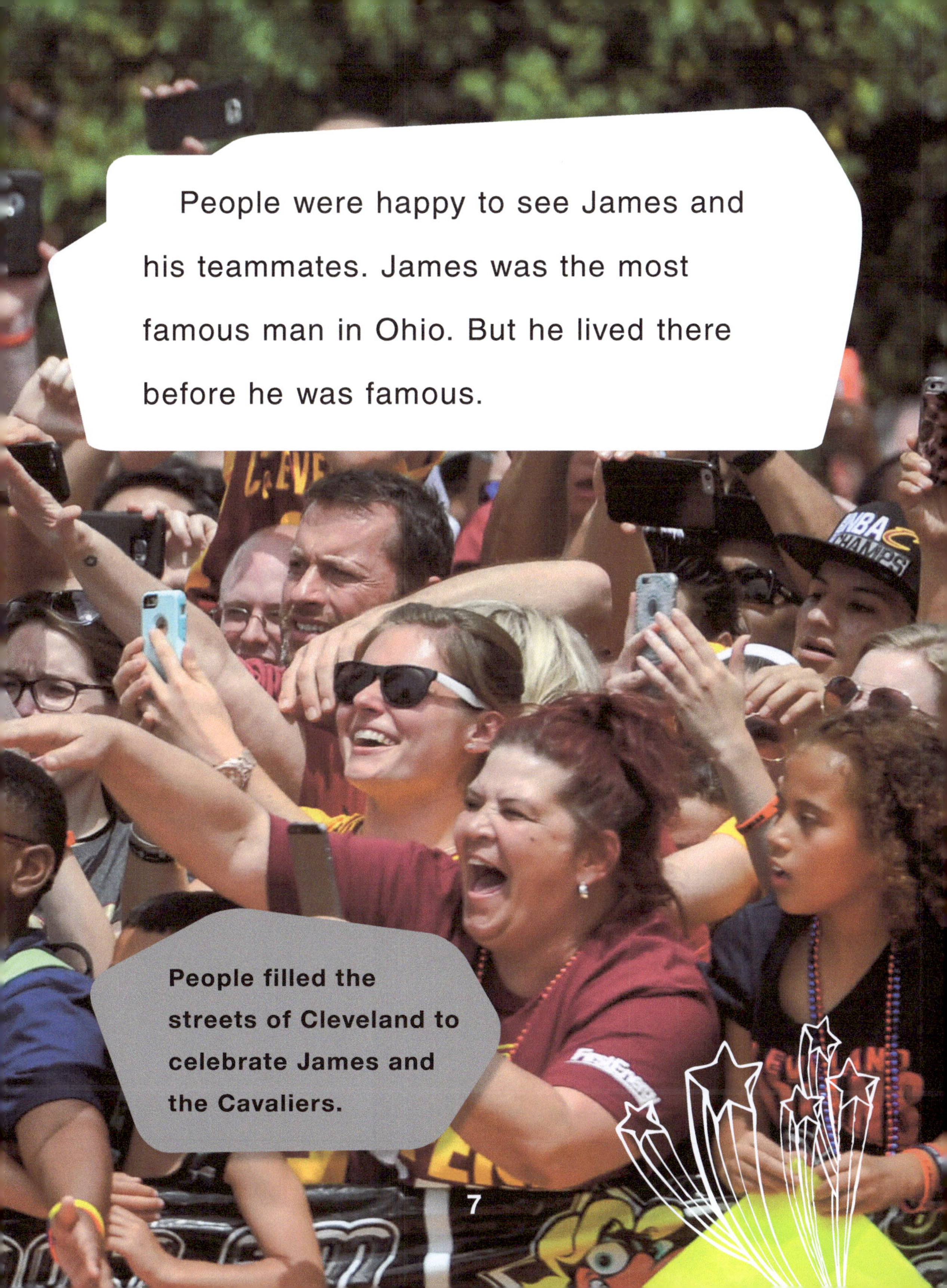

People were happy to see James and his teammates. James was the most famous man in Ohio. But he lived there before he was famous.

People filled the streets of Cleveland to celebrate James and the Cavaliers.

A KID FROM AKRON

James grew up in Akron. It is close to Cleveland. He lived with his mom. He did not know his father.

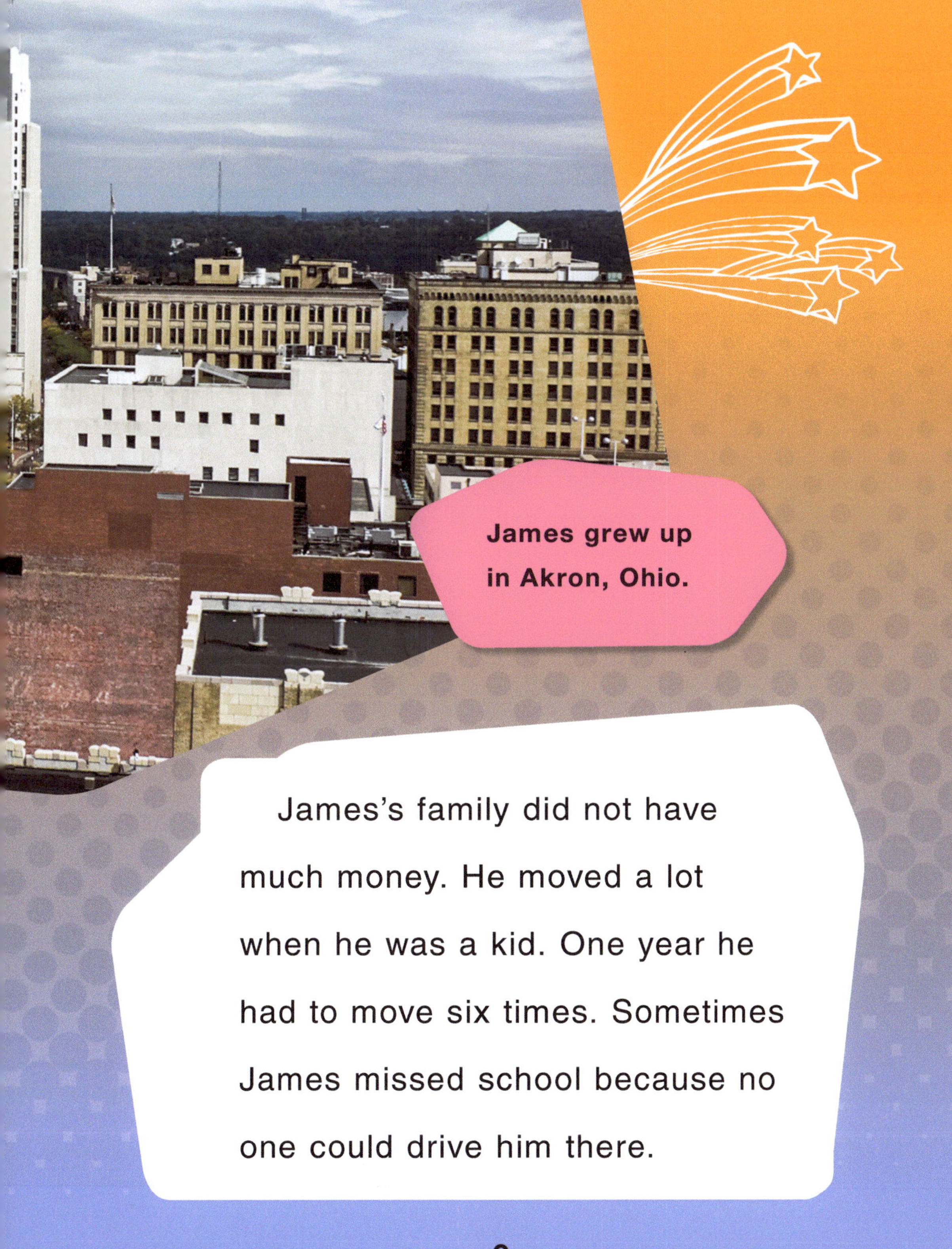

James grew up in Akron, Ohio.

James's family did not have much money. He moved a lot when he was a kid. One year he had to move six times. Sometimes James missed school because no one could drive him there.

James started playing sports in fourth grade. A coach taught him to play basketball. James did not play well at first. But he worked hard and got better. Soon he was one of the best players in his grade.

Every year there was a big basketball game at James's middle school. Students played against teachers. The teachers always won. But when James played, the students won for the first time.

James (second from right) was one of the best basketball players at his middle school.

TWO SPORTS

James played both football and basketball as a kid. He played wide receiver on his high school football team.

IN THE Spotlight

James started high school in 1999. His basketball team won the state championship that school year. Many people watched James. They saw how good he was. They said he could be in the NBA.

James was just a kid who loved basketball. But now he was famous. He was on the covers of sports magazines. Strangers came to his school just to meet him.

James played for St. Vincent-St. Mary High School in Akron.

James (right) got a Cavaliers jersey in 2003 after being drafted by the team.

James did not let this fame change him. He stayed focused. His friends and family loved him. He had a good coach too.

When James finished high school, the NBA was waiting. James was the number one pick in the NBA Draft. The Cleveland Cavaliers chose him. James was happy to play for his hometown.

GOING PRO

James was a great NBA player right away. He scored 25 points in his first game. He won Rookie of the Year in 2004.

In 2007 James led his team to the finals. But they did not win the championship. The same thing happened in 2009. In 2010 James wanted a change. He moved to Florida. He played for the Miami Heat there.

Moving to Miami was a good choice. James won two championships while he played there. He still wanted to get better.

James moved the ball past a Minnesota Timberwolves player in 2004.

James took a shot in a game against the Washington Wizards in 2019.

James spent four seasons in Miami. Then he was ready to go home. He moved back to Cleveland in 2014. He played for the Cavaliers again. That is where he won his third championship. The city was happy to have him back.

In 2018 James looked for another change. He moved to California. He joined the Los Angeles Lakers. The Lakers are one of the most successful teams in the NBA.

SUPERSTAR

James has won the NBA Most Valuable Player (MVP) Award four times.

CHAPTER 3

MORE THAN an Athlete

James is more than a great basketball player. He has **artistic** projects too. In 2015 James started a company that makes movies and TV shows. He has also had small acting **roles**.

James (second from left) stood with the cast of the 2018 movie *Smallfoot*. James was the voice of the character Gwangi.

James (second from left) with his family

SPEAKING OUT

James has also spoken out about **social** issues. With the Miami Heat, he led his team to **protest** against violence. They took a photo together and posted it online. They protested the killing of a young black man named Trayvon Martin. Martin was killed in Florida.

A FAMILY MAN

James is a father and husband. He met his wife in high school. They got married in 2013. They have three kids. James wants to be a good dad.

CHAPTER 4

THE I PROMISE School

James cares about his **community**. When James was a kid, people helped him. Now he wants to be the helper. He wants to help people in Akron.

In 2018 he opened a new school. It is the I Promise School. The school has a lot of teachers. Everyone helps the kids learn. But they help with other things too.

James cares about his hometown, Akron.

James spoke to a crowd outside the I Promise School.

Kids get free meals at the school. They have people to talk to. Even parents and families can get help at the school. James knows that some kids need extra help like he did. He wants to help those kids.

BRAND NEW BIKES

Every student at the I Promise School gets a new bike.

GLOSSARY

artistic
related to art

community
a group of people who live in the same place

parade
people marching together to celebrate something

protest
to speak or act against something

role
a part in a TV show or movie

social
related to people

1984: LeBron James is born on December 30.

1999: James starts high school. That school year, his basketball team wins the state championship.

2003: James plays his first NBA game with the Cleveland Cavaliers on October 29.

2009: James wins his first NBA MVP Award.

2012: James wins his first NBA championship with the Miami Heat.

2016: With the Cleveland Cavaliers, James wins his third championship.

2018: James joins the Los Angeles Lakers.

ACTIVITY

DESIGN YOUR OWN SCHOOL

LeBron James opened a school in his old neighborhood. When he designed the school, he thought about what he needed when he was a kid. He created a school to help other kids like him.

If you could start a school, what kind of school would it be? Think about what might help you as a student. Then make a plan. Create a paper brochure or flyer for your school. You can draw pictures of what your school would look like. You can write about what makes your school special. Share your brochure or flyer with your friends and family.